The Audacity of Heartbreak

Kristina Mahr

Copyright © 2021 Kristina Mahr

All rights reserved.

ISBN-13: 979-8713730000

"It is late now, I am a bit tired; the sky is irritated by stars. And I love you, I love you, I love you — and perhaps this is how the whole enormous world, shining all over, can be created — out of five vowels and three consonants."

- Vladimir Nabokov -

OTHER POETRY COLLECTIONS BY KRISTINA MAHR

It's Only Words

I Wrote You a Poem (I Wrote You Every Poem)

Anyway, I Reach

Something Softer

Say It's the Sea

Heretic Hearts

As Long as It Shines

Without a Scratch

I did not drown in the river I cried, I was baptized in it. You've never seen nothing like me when I'm in love and now you're never going to, I don't promise you much but I promise you're never going to. I come with warnings these days, I come with goddamn warnings. People get a good look at me and say, *I'd hate to see the other guy*, but the other guy walked away without a scratch.

I have soundproofed the room in my chest my heart lives in, so now nobody

can hear it

scream.

All New Songs

There's all new songs on the radio now. I don't
hear any of the ones I used to love you to, not
unless I seek them out and I don't do that
anymore. I called foul anytime someone said it
would get better but it did. It has.

It takes three weeks to break a habit, but
it's been three years and here I am. I guess
loving you is less a thing I do and more a part of
who I am.

Worth

I've come to suspect,
deep down inside,
that you are not worth
this hurt.

Which means, I think,
it's possible, too,
that you were not worth
this love.

Poem Fodder

You are just poem fodder now, certainly not the
love of my life, certainly not the love of the rest
of my life. You know in movies when they run
out of cannonballs and they start shoving scraps
and utensils and whatever they have lying around
into the cannons? That's this. That's you. I ran out
of cannonballs and I'm on to just scraps.

They won't blow anything to pieces, but I promise—

they'll still do some damage.

The Why

To be clear, you are still the who.
I just have no idea about the where.
The when. The how.

The why.

Deep Down

People say that deep down I must
be relieved, deep down I must know
better, deep down I must want more,
but how deep down. I take a flashlight
with me, I dress warmly. I go down,
down, down, into the deepest, darkest
parts of me. I go down, down, down,
and I pause at every landing. To see
if I'm relieved, to see if I know better.
To see if I want more.

But every time I pause—

all I see is I still love you.

All or None

I cry more easily now. Happy, sad, it doesn't matter, I cry more easily now. Missing you is a program inside of me that never stops running, takes up bandwidth, bogs down my memory. I keep it minimized most of the time. I do other things. I know it's there, but look, this is how far I've come, I can do other things. Even laugh, even love, even love someone else. Even try to, I mean, even want to. Even really believe that it's time to.

The trouble is, I'm an all or none of a girl.

And once you give your all away,
all that's left to give is
your none.

Waiting

I am not tired of waiting,
but I am tired of not knowing
what I'm waiting for.

The Only Place

Did you think I'd miss you forever?

(I will miss you forever.)

But this is the only place
I'll say it.

Just Words

These are just words, just words, they're a
dime a dozen, don't cost me a thing to say,
don't cost me a thing to write, I can shout
them, I can spill them, I keep rewriting them,
I keep repeating them.

They are just words, just words.

You know, like the ones you used
to tell me you missed me.

You know, like the ones you used
to tell me you were sorry.

A Mess

Love does not go quietly. I drag it out screaming, holding onto anything it can on its way to the door, like that text where he says that he misses me or that look in his eyes when he asks how I've been. Love howls, digs in its heels and its nails, doesn't get a chance to pack so leaves behind hope, leaves behind want, leaves behind memories.

I can tell you this, love is not getting its security deposit back.

Because love made
a mess of
this place.

On the Roadside

Today so many things are true, I cannot
hold them all. I make some lies, lies, so I
can leave them on the roadside, so I don't
have to carry them anymore, so I don't have
to wonder when they'll turn. I leave your love
for me there, did you know it's there, I visit
it there. I drive past it, circle back around it,
take a picture of it. Someday it won't be
there anymore.

Today so many things are true. I love you,
too. I do not leave that
behind.

Yarn

My body is a vessel for lonely now, a vase, an
urn, a suitcase that has to be checked because
it weighs too much. I have been asked before if
I think you might have done me a favor, giving me
all this hurt like yarn to weave into my
poetry, and I want to be very clear—

you did me no favors.

I don't weave the hurt
into these poems; I weave
what's left of
the love.

How Long

I've never let a dream die before. Never
put it in the attic, closed the door, and let
it starve. I don't know how long it takes, does
anyone know how long it takes.

No, I know, you killed yours differently.

You drove it to the airport and told it

you didn't love it anymore.

Unfinished Business

I've been accusing you of haunting me, and
I'm just writing to say I'm sorry. I'm sorry.
You're not the ghost, I am. Shouting and
you can't hear me. Right in front of you
and you can't see me. This isn't living.
What is this, this isn't living. There's a
bright light at the end of this hallway and
someone said it offers peace, but you're
not there so I'll stay here. I'll stay here.

I'm not sure if my unfinished business is
unloving you or being loved by you.

Either way, I'll never be free of you.

Either way, you'll never be free
of me.

When They Ask Me

When they ask me what happened, I tell them all the things you told me. I say timing, I say distance. I say circumstances, I say it was just too hard. I say it isn't that we don't care about each other, no, it isn't that we don't care about each other.

I tell them all the things you told me.

But in my mind I say,
he didn't think we were worth it.

In my mind I say,
he didn't think I was worth it.

If You Wonder Why

If you wonder why I don't write you anymore, it's because I have run out of ways to say, *you hurt me but I still love you.*

Here, at least, I can pretend it's poetry.

Always Always

You know, if I was happy
then, more often than not
it was because of you.

And if I am happy
now, it is always always

in spite of you.

I Am Not Wrong About This

I have been wrong about
many things, but I am not
wrong about this,
where this is you,
and you are
the love of
my life.

Crushed

We are a boulder on the edge of a cliff; I do
not touch us. We are precarious, above my
head. We are tipping, above my head. We are
a crumpled thing that's turned to stone,
and I do not touch us.

Because if I do, I know—

I am the only one
who's going to get
crushed.

And to Think

And to think,
I called
that love.

My Love Language Must Be
(after Zane Frederick)

ferry rides / I'm sorrys / regardless I want to be with yous / snow globes / road trips / full moons / I don't just think, I knows / text me when you're homes / Labor Day / holding hands / squeezing hands / midnight brushes of his hands / Christmas lights / drunk texts / hey it's mes / my favorite snacks / we cans / we wills / we've got thises / surprise mid-sentence cheek kisses / the opposite of tiptoeing.

(everything but going.)

Your Own Ringtone

You still have your own ringtone in my phone. Your old one, the one that used to mean you were calling to tell me you missed me. The one that used to mean you were calling to tell me you saw something that reminded you of me. The one that one time meant you were calling to tell me you didn't love me anymore.

You still have it, but just because I don't want my hopes to go up any other time my phone rings.

You still have it, but it doesn't matter because

I never

hear it.

Just Another Thing

I wanted to be more
than just another thing
you can't speak about.

Solar Flare

I still love you sometimes. Sometimes,
just sometimes. It's not sunshine
anymore, more like a solar flare.

When it fades, I remember.

Or maybe—

it fades when I

remember.

Irreparable

Somewhere in my medical chart it says loves you, it says was loved by you. It says could've been anyone but is someone who is head over heels for you. It says this is inoperable, it says this is irreparable. It practically says, how could you. It practically says, why would you.

No need for second opinions here.

I already know—
I'm not coming out of this one.

Something That Can Leave You

The trouble is, it stops being a dream
once it comes true.

It becomes something that
can leave you.

Go Ahead and Ask Me

Go ahead and ask me, did I see it coming?
Yes. Was I scared? Yes. Did I stand and greet
it anyway? Yes.

Go ahead and ask me, was it reckless? Yes.
Was I foolish? Yes. Would I do it all again and
again and again? Yes.

Go ahead and ask me, ask me anything, go
ahead and ask me anything.

Anything except that, where the answer is no.

Where the answer is he doesn't.

Where the answer is
he won't.

A Delicate Thing

I was told love would be a delicate thing, so what is this? What is this roaring thing inside of me, this heels dug, fists clenched, *wanting* thing inside of me? What is this thunderstorm inside of me? What is this shipwreck, earthquake, catastrophe inside of me? Why does it shout, why does it demand? Why does it not whisper, why does it not ask? Why does it batter my bones and boil my blood and why does it not go gently and why does it not stay softly and why and why and why—

why does he not want it?

More With You

If this is all we get—my name in the shape of
your laugh, your thumb tracing stars on my
wrist—if this is all we get—me lying in bed in
your shirt, you singing lullabies into the
curve of my neck—if this is all we get—a
sunrise, a ferry ride; a midnight, a beach—

if this is all we get—

no, I know me.

I'd still want more with you.

The Second

You are still
the first person
I think to call.

It's just that,
these days,
I call the second.

This Knowing

I know it's probably hard to hear me say, but
I'm doing fine without you, don't miss a thing
about you, haven't even thought about you
in so long. I know it's probably hard not seeing
my name on your phone, not hearing my voice
telling you sweet things, sweet things, not
seeing me smile my only-for-you smile. I know,
I know, it's probably hard, it's gotta be hard.

This knowing I don't love you anymore.

This knowing you don't have me anymore.

This knowing—

it didn't have to be this way.

The Past

They tell me
to stop living in the past,
but it's the only place
I still live
with you.

Not Here

I am not here for your uncertainty—not when I am certain. I am not here for your distance, your silence, your arms-length—not when I am here, ready, waiting. I am not here for your apologies, and I am even less here for the ones you never gave me—not when I have already forgiven so much. I am not here for your games, your tricks, your half-truths that are more-than-half lies—not when I am naked before you. Not when I have nothing left to hide.

I am not here for your gone.

I am not here for you anymore.

I Will Not

I may have wasted my time
on you, but I swear to God I will
not waste my life on you.

The World is Ending

The world is ending and nothing's changed. I call and you don't answer. Sirens blare and I turn the volume all the way up on my phone in case you call me back. The sky is on fire and I brush ashes from my lashes as I wonder where you are. The earth opens up beneath my feet and I have to choose which side to stand on. I think you're west, so I choose west. I watch the other side drift farther and farther away and pray I've chosen right.

The world is ending and nothing's changed—

you are the first thing on my mind.

(You are the last thing on my mind.)

Dormant

Love is sleeping inside of me, lying dormant, keeping so still I forget it's there, I keep forgetting it's there. It's dust-covered, cobwebbed, peaceful, at peace.

But I'm no fool.

I know it's still there.

I know it's just waiting.

(Waiting for you to wake it.)

You Would

If you could go back in time and
change this, I believe you would.

I don't believe you would unhurt me.

I believe you would
unlove me.

I'll Run Again

I'm fine more often than not these days, and that isn't even a lie. I look for constellations in the Christmas lights shining in on my bedroom ceiling instead of only ever thinking about how much you hated projector lights. I sing along to songs I used to have to skip. I don't bring you up in conversations just to feel your name on my tongue, just to hear it in the air. This is healing, I tell myself. This is the doctor saying it's getting better, even though there are screws and bolts holding parts of me together. Even though I still get tired easily, even though I need an ice pack at the end of most days. This is the doctor promising me I'll run again, and me starting to believe her.

I'll run again.

(Just not to you.)

All for You

I would have
traded it all
for you.

(Thank god I didn't trade it all for you.)

When Something Hurts

All I can think about when something hurts
is why didn't I appreciate it more all the times
it didn't.

When my head hurts, when I pull
a muscle, when I catch a cold.

When you don't love me anymore.

Be Kind

They say to be kind, for everyone
is fighting a difficult battle.

Be kind.

(I am fighting not to love you.)

Who Will

If I fade away, who will find me. Who will notice my edges start to blur. Who will reach a hand out to make sure it doesn't pass right through me. Who will know I have been quiet for too long. Who will look for me in the places I used to be. Who will want to.

I am not afraid of being forgotten when I'm gone.

I am afraid of being forgotten while I'm here.

What Would You Do

I would never tattoo someone's name on me, but I would tattoo your thumbprint on the curve of my hip. I would tattoo your lifeline across the palm of my own hand. I would tattoo your constellation two inches south of my collarbone where I could hand-to-heart wish on it on every exhale, when all of the stars fall.

What would you do if you knew
there was no chance you would ever
regret it?

I would love you.

I would love you.

So Much More

I spent so much time saying

I need so much more than that

that it's taken me 'til now to realize—

I need so much more than you.

The Poor Souls

What am I thanking the stars for if not the calluses on
your fingertips? What is even the point of any of it,
any bit of it, if I'm not including the way your
forearms look with your sleeves pushed back in
my nightly prayers? How does anyone, least of all
me, write poetry and not mention the sliver of skin
that appears when you reach up to scratch the back
of your neck and your shirt rides up? I flip page after
page in book after book and somehow nobody has
paused mid-sentence to touch upon the exhale of
your laugh and what it does against my skin, and I
do not understand it, I do not understand
it, except to think, perhaps—

they must not have loved you.

The poor souls, they must not
have been loved by you.

Are You Coming Back

The house is burning down and I am doing my hair. Curling it carefully, deliberately, squinting at my reflection through the smoke. I fan my face to keep my makeup from dripping off in the heat. I take off my new red dress when the edge of it catches fire and kick it over to one corner, annoyed that I already cut the tags off and can't return it. Would they have taken it singed? If I said it came that way? If I was willing to accept store credit? It's one of those things I'll never get the chance to know.

Are you coming back with the extinguisher soon, love. Are you coming back with the buckets, with the hose.

Are you coming back, the house is burning down around me.

Are you coming back.

Is It?

I am still trying to forget you.

(Is this poetry yet?)

Instead of Peace

Love is a fight I've been picking with you for years now. You sharpen your sword against the way I cling to you in my sleep, and I wake up with surrenders in my mouth. I spit them in the sink before I kiss you. Nobody said this would be easy, and it isn't. It won't be.

But you could aim for my heart, and you don't.

And I could aim for your head, but I won't.

Instead of *I love yous* we exchange *do you still love mes*.

Instead of peace you bring me

joy.

Tomorrow

Tomorrow didn't tell me for sure that it was coming but shows up anyway, ragged at the edges, hungover from the night before. It waits for me to say something, but I am busy looking at pictures of Yesterday, busy remembering Yesterday, busy wishing for wishing for wishing for Yesterday.

I know I should be happy to see it. I know I should be grateful to see it.

But it keeps showing up alone, when—

I keep hoping it'll bring you.

So I Walk

My heart brakes. That is not a typo, it slams its
foot down on the pedal so hard I fly through the
windshield. I am more bruise than love now, more
splintered glass than want now. By the time I get back
up again, you have taken the key from the ignition.
The key you put in there, the first one to ever fit, the
first one to ever start it. You throw it in the reeds,
somewhere neither of us can find it. You don't look,
but I do, though it gets harder and harder to want to.

So I walk. I walk, no heart to drive me.

I walk, no love to
guide me.

What I Mean

When I say that my life
is worse off for having
loved you,

what I mean is that my life
is worse off for having
lost you.

Goldilocks

You were Goldilocks, and I was too hot, too cold. Too hard, too soft. Too much, too little; too here, too gone; too this, too that; never just right, never just right, but you know what? It doesn't matter what you think because—

I was never really yours.

My To-Do List

I pad my to-do list with things I know I can cross off easily. I write *get out of bed*. I write *brush my hair, brush my teeth*. I write *walk the dogs*.

Check, check, check.

I write *breathe*, because I can do that. Even on my worst of days, I can do that.

One easy thing to cross off.

But then I think of something even easier.

So I write *miss him*.

It's the first thing I check off each day.

Champagne Promises

We are a product of champagne promises that fell out of the cab on the drive home. I like to think some other couple found them. I like to think there are two people out there who will for the rest of their lives tell the story of the night they found everything, everything abandoned on the side of the road. I like to think they spare a thought for us now and then and wonder whose loss became their gain.

When we get home, you pat down your pockets, and I check beneath the lipstick in my purse.

We come up empty-handed.

I like to think they aren't fools.

They who keep that which fools made.

Anywhere, Anything, Anyone

Where would you go if you could go anywhere?
What would you do if you could do anything?
Who would you be if you could be anyone?

I would go to you.

I would love you.

I would be someone who loves you, no—

I would be someone who's loved
by you.

There Was a Time

There was a time I loved you, in the past now, a yesterday three years ago. We would go for our long walks around the frozen ponds of my wounds, and you would fish inside of them while I sat and shivered in a dreamworld of warm words. You'd come home with fresh ways to hurt me and I'd come home with more holes drilled in the ice of me. We'd sit by the fire and watch the cold spill from my bones, and you would have the nerve to call me frigid.

There was a time I loved you.

But there was never a time you deserved it.

So Much Space

You took up so much space in my heart, and I
haven't rearranged it since you. Everything else is
still pushed up against the walls. Someone said I
should use this space to dance, but there is no
music in here, just echoes of the things we meant
to say softly, the things we never meant to say at all,
the things I thought I would have a chance to say
later. Was my heart always this big? It feels bigger
now, emptied of you. Later I think this will be
a good thing.

But for now, it is drafty in here.

For now, I hate every inch of the space
that wasn't enough
to hold you.

Swept Up

I have been swept up before, but only
under the rug, never off my feet.

I remember loving you.

Surely there have been wars with less blood shed.

There were early days when he had to straighten my
fingers from the claws I thought love required them
to be, but now I am all soft things. A pillow, where he
rests his head on my lap and I write a poem for every
one of his eyelashes. A blanket, where I cover his
body with mine in the middle of the night and he
makes shadow puppets in the moonlight. A feather,
where he swears nothing I give him is too heavy, not
half of the weight on my shoulders, not the love you
did not want.

Our floors are bare, there are no rugs here.

I am swept up, and I think—

I only loved you at my worst.

I love him at my best.

Forgive Me

Forgive me, I keep thinking about how many horses died at war. They never asked to be there. Did they even know that they were being led to battle. Did they even know that they could rebel and turn and run. Forgive me, I keep thinking about the way things shouldn't be. It doesn't matter that they are, they shouldn't be, and that keeps me up most nights. Forgive me, I keep thinking about whether I would know the difference between a sunrise and a sunset if I did not know the time. Can I tell a beginning from an ending. Would one bring hope and one bring sadness or would I see beauty in them both.

Forgive me, I keep thinking about you.

You always knew that you could run.

Try As I Might

I write poems in which
you love me, but try
as I might, I cannot
write them
true.

A Buffer, A Barrier

I don't know how to hold this hurt. It's all sharp corners and jagged edges, splintered and endlessly splintering. So I wrap it in anger, which isn't soft, but it's something, you know, it's something between me and the hurt. A buffer, a barrier. Something to muffle the cries of the hurt so I can finally sleep at night. Anger doesn't rage, anger doesn't roar, anger *simmers*. Anger holds my hand and escorts me up over the barbed wire hurt to a place where I can say your name without any of me breaking.

Maybe if I was stronger, I could hold the hurt without the anger.

But maybe if *you* were stronger—

I wouldn't have to hold either.

Repeat the Sounding Joy

They sing *repeat the sounding joy*, and I think, yes. Yes, repeat it. Yes, the joy, the sounding joy, repeat it. One year from now and two years from now and thirty years from now I still want to be woken up too early on Christmas morning because he wants to tell me that it snowed. He wants to hold my hand as the world is quiet, blanketed white, as we are the first two people to mark it with our footprints. For a little while, they will say, *we were here*. For a little while, they will say, *it was just us and the quiet world, he woke me so I wouldn't miss it*.

Repeat the sounding joy.

Repeat it.

Repeat it.

Our Story

If I wrote our story, I don't think any editor would buy it. I think they'd ask, "Why did he leave her?" and I'd have to admit that I don't know. I think they'd say, "Well surely there were signs he was thinking about going," and I'd have to say trust me, I've looked, there weren't. I think they'd wonder, "Isn't three years too long for her to still be in love with him?" and I'd have to tell them it might be, yes, it might be, but that doesn't mean it's unrealistic.

I think they'd want my character to move on at a certain point, to fall in love with someone new, someone better. I think they'd want her to live happily ever after even if it wasn't with him.

But I don't know how to write that ending.

I don't know how to live that ending.

Things That Used to Be Walls

You leveled me, I think you should know you leveled me. I had to rebuild myself from scratch, and the trouble is, I had to start right away. I couldn't go around all scrap metal and crumbled bricks, all plaster and two-by-fours and things that used to be walls. I just had to start building. I had to start where I was and use what I had.

Do you understand, do you see?

I didn't have time to wait, I didn't have time to make

my foundation anything but

missing you.

Wouldn't You Know

Wouldn't you know,
the only thing harder than
being with you
is
not being with you.

A Pocket of Air

All loving you does these days is break my heart. I live in a cave now, and it's filled to the brim with water, so every day I choose whether to drown or to hold my breath. There's not much living in either. Sometimes I find pockets of air and I forget for a second or two that everything else for me is cold and wet and gasping, but those pockets are too small to build a life around.

I read through all of our old texts last night, and I wanted to ask you if you remember loving me.

I wanted to ask you because I had forgotten and I thought maybe you did too.

It was a pocket of air until I remembered I couldn't ask, and now—

I'm drowning again.

I Can't Escape You

When I say I can't escape you, what I mean is I run upstairs instead of out the front door. What I mean is everyone's shouting at the screen and calling me a fool. What I mean is they all say I had it coming when you catch up to me.

When I say I can't escape you, what I mean is I don't try to.

What I mean is I don't want to.

Planted Dreams

You can't just toss seeds onto the hard packed dirt and wait for something to grow. You need to bury them. You need to water them. You need to make sure the light can reach them.

What I'm saying is, I have planted dreams inside this heartbreak.

Deep down inside the cracks of it.

I am watching them grow.

Maybe I Was Right

The world didn't end. Isn't that something?
Nobody holding my hand and still I stand. Isn't
that something? We are such brittle, boneless
things, always fighting for what we want and
never what we have. This isn't something. This
isn't something.

This is you saying the universe is chaos.

This is me saying the universe is for us.

In the middle of the night, you said
that maybe I was right.

This is a memory you don't have anymore.

This is a memory I don't want anymore.

A Waiting

What is love but
the first shoe dropping.

What is love but
a waiting
for
the other one.

What It's Supposed To

Do not call my heart soft. Do not call it fragile or bruised or weak. Do not call it broken, don't you dare call it broken. It is doing what it's supposed to. It is pumping blood and pounding pounding pounding it is keeping me alive.

It is strong, my heart is strong, my heart is doing what it's supposed to.

It is loving you.

And it is working

on no longer

loving you.

Poetry Doesn't Care

Poetry won't dance with me. It won't laugh at
my jokes, not even a pity laugh, not even a roll
of its eyes. Poetry won't pick up the phone when
it's late at night and I'm trying to find my car in
the parking lot. Poetry doesn't care that I'm
scared. Poetry never whispers sweet things
in my ear, never wakes me up in the middle
of the night just because it misses the sound
of my voice, has not once told me it loves me.

But then again

neither did

you.

Threadbare

My love for you is a threadbare security blanket
with too many holes in it to keep me warm.

But I still hold it tight.

I still don't know how
to sleep
without it.

Next

I haven't stopped loving you, but
I've stopped believing in you.

So I'm thinking
love is
next.

Mime on a City Street Corner

We pass a mime on a city street corner, and I stop and watch and wonder if he truly believes he's in a box. Nothing but air around him, but he pushes his hands against walls only he can see as though he's trapped, as though he's cornered, as though there's no escape. He mouths words we cannot hear, and I wonder if he thinks he's shouting, I wonder if he thinks he's screaming.

I wonder if he's drowning in there, in this box no one else can see, the one he seems to think
is real.

I wonder if he's drowning and you—
you are not watching, are you?

You are not watching.

Untouched Snow

An untouched snow of a year
thus far, unsullied by
your footprints.

Don't come this way, don't
walk this way, I ask of
you, I beg of you.

You can see from afar that it
is beautiful.

You do not have
to ruin it.

A Lake Somewhere

There are flowers that go their whole lives without ever being seen. Trees that never once get climbed. Sand that never becomes a castle. Stars that fall without a single wish upon them. Books that get printed but never opened, never read. Songs sung, recorded on a cassette that no one ever listens to. There is a lake somewhere, I'm sure of it, that no one has ever swum in. A mountain that's never been climbed and so, a view that has never been taken.

What I'm saying is, thank you for seeing me.

What I'm saying is, thank you
for loving me.

So Long

I don't regret asking the question.

But I do regret spending so long
thinking you're the answer.

Like an Anvil

I hope I hang over your head. Like an icicle. Like an anvil. Like a bell, a ringing bell, I hope in quiet moments you never can find peace. Kept up by my hope in your head. Kept up by my voice in your bed. You wake up reaching for me, for apologies, but you never find either. Truth is, you won't find one without the other. Not anymore, I swear. Not anymore.

I hope it haunts you, drives you mad, in the opposite of all the ways I used to.

You know, my number hasn't changed.

But I have.

Threw Out

I threw out the way you said my name.

I kept most everything else,
but I could not keep that,
and I could not keep your arms around me,
and I will probably regret this later,
but I could not keep your laugh.

I swear, I swear,
I kept everything else,
I kept
almost
everything else.

(I threw out the way I love you, too.)

(I had to part with that.)

Any Greater

I have fallen
for lesser men than you.

But I have never fallen
for any greater.

The Audacity of Heartbreak

I am here to speak to the audacity. The audacity!
The audacity of love, for starters. The sheer
audacity of love, which is to say nothing of
the audacity of heartbreak, let us say nothing
of the audacity of heartbreak. Oh no, and the
audacity of dreams? The absolute audacity of
dreams! And of course the audacity of beauty—
moreover, the audacity of sunrises. The audacity
of the ocean, such a thing, the unfathomable
audacity of the ocean. And can you even
comprehend the audacity of the moon? Of
the stars? Of the blue of the night sky? I
cannot, I tell you, I can absolutely not, but
nonetheless I find myself before the audacity
of joy. Of happiness? Yes, I suppose it falls to
me to speak to the audacity of happiness

and how I was in love once (the audacity of love)
beneath the silver moon (the audacity of the moon)
and held your hand in mine (the audacity

of heartbreak.)

Plenty of Fish

I've been fishing in this well of hurt again. Cold night, no stars, I've been fishing, and the fishing's good. I don't think this is what they meant when they said there's plenty of fish in the sea, but they'd have been right, plenty of fish in *this* sea. Some bigger than others. Some that take some wrestling to get up, but you know me, never one to back down from a fight. I spend no small amount of time wrestling my hurts. Should be near out of them I'd think, but I catch and release, so I keep pulling up the same hurts, again and again. You don't have to tell me I'm a fool. You don't have to tell me.

Cold night, no stars.

You don't have to tell me the sun is up, the sun is shining.

You don't have to tell me

he's never coming back.

In a Crowd

I looked for you in a crowd today. You weren't in it, but you could've been. So many people, you could've been. What would I have done had I seen you? I don't know how to say hello to you anymore. We are not made for small talk, you and I. None of our talk has ever been small. It has always put mountains to shame, it has always been the stuff of skyscrapers, and now what, I'd say hello? Hello, it's nice to see you, how have you been? It would not be nice to see you. Nice is too tame a word for what it would be to see you. And how have you been? Do I really want to know how you have been? Do I want to risk hearing you're happy? Do I want to risk knowing you're happy without me?

In the end it's for the best
you were not in that crowd today.

But still I wish you had been.

If Given the Chance

How do you get over the things you are still buried beneath? The things you'd call regrets if you weren't sure you'd do them all over again if given the chance. If given the chance. If given the chance what am I supposed to say, that I would love you less? Why would I. Why should I. I loved the amount I loved. I loved the way I loved. That it is now bricks piled high upon my chest is less regret and more kismet.

Sometimes love breaks.

And sometimes only one of us
gets out before it does.

Sisyphus

When I am feeling noble—and lying to
myself—I declare that we were Sisyphus
and love was our boulder.

When I am feeling vengeful—and still lying
to myself—I contend that I was Sisyphus
and you were the boulder.

When I am feeling introspective—and tired of lying
to myself—I admit that I was both Sisyphus
and the boulder.

When I am feeling tired—and brutally honest
with myself—I acknowledge that I was and ever am
all three of Sisyphus, the boulder, and the mountain.

I am the carrier of my burdens.

I am the burden.

And I am the thing
that I must overcome.

Just Fine

I'm doing just fine. I've peeled your hands from my hips and your voice from my mind and I'm doing just fine. All of those promises you made, now I know you aren't keeping them and I'm doing just fine. There was a peak, wouldn't you know there was a peak, look hurt's on its way down the other side and I'm doing just fine. One foot in front of the other like this, like whoa, like I'm doing just fine, because I am, I'm—

what's that? Oh

no I know you didn't ask.

Trust me, I know

you didn't ask.

Ten Thousand Piece Puzzle

Trust is a painting I gave you that you returned as a ten thousand piece puzzle. I have been trying to put it back together for months now, but—am I mistaken or is it missing pieces? I think it's missing pieces. Truth be told, I don't even remember what it's supposed to look like. Was it beautiful, before you broke it? Did you treasure it, before you tore it?

Sometimes someone else comes along and helps me fit a piece or two, but mostly I work on it on my own.

It will be whole again.

But it will never be yours again.

Darkness

They said if we shot for the moon,
we would at least land among the stars.

But we didn't.

All we landed amid
was darkness.

Because It's Sad

What if the sky is blue because it's sad.

What if the times the sunset paints it pink—when we all stop and take a picture of it that never does it justice—is the sky experiencing a rare moment of joy.

Do you think it makes it even sadder
that we only clap for it when it's happy.

That when night falls we marvel
at the stars that shine within
and never stop to notice the
dark spaces in between.

But no, I'm being sentimental—the sky is blue for scientific reasons.

Just like hearts don't really break.

They keep beating.

Both You and Peace

I had to draw a line
in the sand.

And I'm sorry
that I could not find a way
to have both you
and peace
on my side of it.

How Was I Supposed to Know

There is a song that I love that I love that I love
that I think I love because you never know when
it's over and over and over again it fades and
seconds of silence pass and pass me by and I
think that's why I think it's done it's over it's
gone but then it comes back it builds back up
and the music swells and you forget there
ever was silence 'til it happens again
and again and again and again it
happens again.

But eventually it *does* end.

It really does end.

How was I supposed to know
that this time it really did end.

For as Long as I Can

Cacti can survive up to two years without
water. They store the water inside and pull
from their reserves for as long as they can.

For as long as they can.

I will love you for as long as I can.

But it's been years
since you gave me any love
and my reserves

are

low.

Something to Be Remembered

We spoke silence, we danced stillness. This is how I will remember us when we are something to be remembered—as lonely together, as hopelessly hopeful. As never more gone than when we were here. As listening with our hands over our ears. As irreverently worshipful, as wholly broken.

Someday I will remember how indifferently you loved me.

But for today I try to forget the way you hold me like you're letting me go.

On My Wall

I don't flip houses, but I flip words. You say you miss me, and I rip out the period and replace it with an exclamation point. I slide it back a little bit, though, so I can add a "so much." I change it to all caps. I stretch each letter to ten feet tall. I italicize it, I underline it. I polish it, I frame it.

By the time I ask you about it, you've already forgotten you ever said it.

And I

have hung it

on

my wall.

Reappraised

I sold my love to you so cheaply because
you convinced me that was the most
I would ever get for it.

I got it reappraised.

Turns out
you can't
afford it.

Guarantees

I've been looking for miracles like this isn't one, just this, just you and me and Cassiopeia burning bright in the sky above us. What am I even looking for that is not here, between us, around us. Why am I so scared of tomorrow when today you make my name hold more meaning than any baby name book has ever attributed to it. When today I love you more than I did yesterday, though yesterday I know I told you I could not love you more.

Maybe I haven't been looking for miracles so much as I've been looking for promises.

No, I know you promised.

Maybe I haven't been looking for promises so much as I've been looking for
guarantees.

A Race

I have the flight booked before you finish the question. I'm in my car before we hang up the phone. I run every red light, and I'm on the plane within an hour. The pilot comes on the intercom and says the wind's in our favor, and I'm grateful, oh, I'm grateful. I have no luggage to pick up because I didn't stop and pack, so I run from the plane to the first cab I see. I'm in front of your house, I'm on your porch, I'm ringing your bell, I'm waiting for you to answer.

I'm waiting to see if I was fast enough this time.

It's always a race between me and your mind.

It's always a race between me—

and you changing it.

Every Day

I chose to love you.

Every day, I chose to love you.

And now, every day,
I have to choose
not to.

Even the Bad Ones

I won't still love you in the morning.

All good things must come to an end, and so must all bad things. Don't ask me which we were.

You know, I fall in love in all my dreams.

Even the bad ones.

Those are the ones
where I fall in love
with you.

Imagine If

Imagine if we all called that love. If the sweetest love song ever written was about a man who every now and then decides to answer a woman's texts. If sonnets were written about a man who came back to her over and over again (after he left her over and over again.) If we all went to the theaters to swoon over a woman falling in love with a man who spends more time looking at his phone than at her. If the most romantic wedding vows involved the groom apologizing for making the bride cry again, again, again, all the while both knowing he'll do it again, again, again.

Imagine if that was the pinnacle, the highest height our hearts could reach, the most we could ever hope for.

Maybe then
I would have
stayed.

Still Waiting

I am still waiting for a goodbye.

For you to say you're sorry,
and for me to pretend I mean it
when I say that it's okay.

Least Of All Me

Truth be told,
what makes this easy
is I had the chance to see
how you won't fight
for anything you love,
least of all
me.

Love Wins

Love wins.

I mean in a fight between me and love, love wins.

It has to be said, love fights dirty. Love shouts all night long so I wake up tired. Love spreads from my head to my toes—throbs in my throat, bubbles in my lungs; falters my footsteps, tangles in my hair. I can't shake it off, can't wash it off, you know love is sticky business.

Love makes me miss the train sometimes. Makes me miss my turn, makes me miss my stop, makes me miss, makes me miss.

Every time I think love's down, it gets back up swinging. Every time I think love's weak, it lifts me bodily, carries me, *show off*, I think, *show off*.

Love wins.

But it turns out,
that doesn't mean
I lose.

Instead I Know

Look, I would have been worried if
this heartbreak didn't hurt.

It would mean I was mistaken.

It would mean I never loved you.

Instead, I know I wasn't.

Instead, I know

I did.

Guessing

There's no excuse, but I'm guessing you have one.
I'm guessing its creases have gone soft by now from
all the times you've folded and unfolded it. Not to
show me, no, I haven't earned the right to see, but
I'm guessing you show it to your guilt any time it
speaks up.

I'm guessing, I'm guessing, all I'm doing is guessing.

I'm guessing you're not coming back. I'm
guessing you think it's better this way. I'm
guessing you're sorry, and

I could forgive you, I could forgive you, I could
forgive it all, except—

I cannot forgive
that I have to keep

guessing.

I Wish You Really Had It

I wish you really had it. My heart, I mean, my heart. I wish you had it like a fish in a tank, where you could see what makes it struggle, where you could see what makes it thrive. Where you could see the way it beats harder when you're near. The way it pounds, the way it races. And where you could see the bruises. The cracks, the holes, the blood. The hurt, I wish you could see the hurt, I wish you had to see the hurt.

I wish you really had it.

And I really wish
you didn't.

Three for Three

Past, present, future,
there was a time you were
three for three.

But from this point on,
you will only ever have
one of those
with me.

Small

Some people like me small. Like me sidecar-sized, got me sidekick-prized, some people don't like a voice they can't talk over. And I'm good at small, don't get me wrong, I'm good at small, good at quiet, good at cupping my hands to give someone a boost. It's just that lately I've found myself outgrowing the tidy little box some people like me in. It's just that lately I've found an echo tucked into my voice, how long has that been in there, how long has it been waiting to boom. And oh, it's taken a liking to ricocheting, it's taken a liking to flying, and I've taken a liking to the force of it coming back to me.

Some people like me small, but I see now that *they're* small.

I see that I've
outgrown them.

Over This

I joke that my therapist picks up her pen every time I say your name. That she's keeping a tally of how many times I say it. It might be in the hundreds, is probably in the thousands. If she's tired of it, she doesn't let on, she can't let on, which is why that's the only place I still say it.

Nobody else wants to hear it. Nobody else wants my heart to still be broken. Some of that is kindness I'm sure, but some of it isn't.

Can I blame them? I probably can't blame them.

I want me
to be over this too.

Not One

I wanted to tell you so many things.

And not one of those things
was goodbye.

Outlier

You break the curve. I grade all other
loves against you but you're an outlier—
I loved you too much, too long, too
hard. Nobody else stands a chance
when I measure them against you.

I am not saying you ruined love for me.

But I am saying
you ruined me
for love.

Meant to Be

I know that we
were meant to be,
but it's hard for me to believe
we were meant to be
this.

Everything Everything

And when I find you—when you find me—when we find each other, I do not think the stars will fall. I doubt the birds will break out in song, and the clouds are unlikely to part. The world won't stop turning, the waves won't stop breaking, the sun will not stop setting. We won't stop aging, we won't stop changing, there is no chance we will stop wanting.

But when I find you—when you find me—when we find each other—

everything will be different.

Everything everything will
be different.

My Own

February is calling, and if I answer, I'm convinced it will have your voice. Convinced by whom? By hope, by heartsick hearts—my own. I claim it—bold, like that, *my own*—though I did not discover all of it. I will give credit where credit is due and put your initials on some parts. Some corners. Some calluses, some chasms, some cliffs. Not all of them are shadow; some are awash with light.

February is calling, and I have no choice but
to answer.

I mean, I have a choice and I choose to make it.

When I tell you I found joy, I mean
I opened my eyes and it was there.

Not Even

Heartbreak is no cure for love.

(Not even a very big heartbreak.)

And love is no cure for heartbreak.

(Not even a very big love.)

The Big Bang

I believe in love at first sight in
the same way I believe in
the Big Bang theory.

From nothing, there was something.

There was everything.

But we are never not aware
that someday
there may be nothing
again.

My Tricky Love

My love, my tricky love. It snuck into your heart one night through a side door when your guard was down and your hands were everywhere, my love, my tricky love. When you realized, you slammed the door, but it was still inside, my love, my tricky love.

Do you feel it in there, wandering. Do you feel it in there, wanting. I do not call it home; I could not even if I tried.

It is lost in there, inside of you.

I hope it warms something
inside of you.

Still

I still call you everything, and you

still don't call me.

Gone With the Wind

I took up running the day you left. You
could say you inspired me, speeds like that,
gone with the wind like that, you could say
you inspired me. What else could you say,
what else would you say, what else do you
choose not to say.

I said I couldn't say goodbye to you again.

But I didn't mean
you should leave
without giving me
the chance to.

Sticks and Stones

The words that cost you
nothing to say
cost me everything
to hear.

So Incomplete

Don't you do that. Don't you pretend like I built us from thin air. Not when you handed me the materials. Not when you told me to start building, that you were on your way. Not when my fingertips are calloused, my knees and elbows bruised, my heart so incomplete, so incomplete, so goddamn incomplete.

Don't you do that, don't you dare do that.

Don't you dare

pretend

you didn't

love me.

Hard to Get

To be clear,
the only time
I play hard to get
is when I do not want
to be gotten.

Can You Believe It

Somebody wants to keep me, can you believe it? I know, I know, it sounds like a lie but he told me, he told me he wants to keep me. Like I am something worth keeping, like he does not want to lose me. Can you believe it? He said he knows he doesn't deserve me and I know, I know you said that too, but unlike you he didn't use it as an excuse to break my heart. No, he used it as an excuse to love me harder, he keeps loving me harder, can you believe it, he keeps loving me harder.

He holds me like if everything was falling I am the one thing he would catch.

Can you believe it?

No, I know
you can't.

Formative Memory

Your hands open so easily, I want to
ask how you do that. I used to know. Once
when I was four my dad was pushing me on
a tire swing and for a split second my hands
forgot they were supposed to hold on. It
was a lot like flying until I hit the wooden
beam and I guess you can call that a formative
memory because now my hands don't open,
my hands never open. Now I hold on for dear
life. Now I do not want the hurt of open hands.

My hands don't understand that sometimes,
keeping them closed hurts worse.

No Blood

I thought this grief was an open
wound, but there is no blood—only
an echo of your laugh, only a shadow
of your smile, only a glimmer of your touch.

Which is to say it is every exquisite thing and
my hands just passing through them.

I tell myself, *it cannot touch me so it cannot hurt me*, but

I cannot touch it so it
destroys me.

It Is

I don't love you anymore.

I wouldn't have thought of that as
poetry, but in this, it is.

It is.

Memories Included

House for sale, fully furnished, memories included!

Beautiful granite countertops on which I sat and read him crossword clues while he made me pancakes. Dark wood floors—unscratched!—where he spun me 'round and 'round while old Bee Gees records played. (Records also included!) Comfy black sofa where he first told me he loved me, complete with two gorgeous purple pillows I cried into months later when he changed his mind. (Don't worry, no damage!) (No damage to the pillows, I mean, no damage to the pillows.) Working electric fireplace guaranteed to warm your bones, but it might not warm your heart, it shows no sign of warming hearts. The bed, you can have the bed, I have nothing to say about the bed except it has four posts, a mattress, I drown in it, I've drowned in it. Garage fits two cars, but it fits one even better, don't worry, it fits one even better.

I hope it brings you joy, I hope you
burn it to the ground.

(I should have. I should have.)

Just Like That

I know a goodbye when I see one.

(Now, I do now, I didn't but I do now.)

I know it's saying all the right things. I know it's
handing out hope like flower bouquets, big and
beautiful and blooming. I know it's sweet, I know it's
sparkling, I know it's something I'm going to write
about in my journal that night like *this*, like *this*, like
this is everything I've ever wanted.

I know it's joy, I know it's happiness.

And I know that the next minute,
just like that,
it isn't.

A Blessing

'No feeling lasts forever'
used to be a thing
that scared me.

Now it is
a blessing.

If You're Looking

I will leave this here like a slip of paper that's just fallen out of my pocket, where you could find it if you're looking. I will not send it to you. I will not address it to you. You'll only have to guess that it's to you, that it's for you.

When I write that I still dream you. When I write that I still miss you. When I write that every now and then I'm still half-convinced I love you.

I'm leaving it here, where you could find it if you're looking.

Are you looking?

Forbid Me

Somebody told me I am
allowed to miss him, and
I do not need permission,
no, I do not need permission.

(Tell me I can't miss him.)

(Forbid me from missing him.)

Needle & Thread

The pen is the needle,
the words are the thread.

It will heal, but first
it will hurt.

From the Jaws of Catastrophe

Not all love poems fall sweetly, land softly. I have
borrowed this one from the jaws of catastrophe,
and it did not come easily. Nor readily. Nor
willingly. If you look closely, you'll still find chaos
in its eyes, wanton wanting in its smile. There are
days I think the bitter wholly leaves the sweet behind.

Forgive me, I meant to write of flowers, and here
I talk of thorns. But this is still a love poem. This
is still a love poem.

I have lashed the words together like the
pieces of my heart, and I risk these fragile
things, I risk these fragile things, I have
the nerve to call them

beautiful.

I Did Not Know

Loving you is like the first time I looked up at
the night sky in the middle of nowhere
after a lifetime of only seeing it
through city lights.

I did not know the world held this, that it has
held this all this time.

But now I'll know, I'll never not
know, even when I'm back beneath those
city lights—

I'll never not know this world holds magic.

Always Going, Always Gone

In my head, time stopped for you when we did. You will always be the age you were. You will always have that one streak of grey, and your hair will always be a little shorter than you'd like. You will always wear that sweatshirt anytime it's chilly. You will always roll your eyes like that, you'll always laugh like that, you'll always have plans drawn up and laying on your kitchen table for what your backyard will be, but it won't be that yet. You'll always have paint color options all over your wall, but it won't be any of them yet.

You'll always be going, always going, always gone, and I—

I will always be missing you.

I will always be missing you.

(I guess time stopped for both of us.)

Your World

This hurt has your name.

You always wanted to leave your mark on this world, is this how you wanted to leave it? As crumpled up pages on some girl's bedroom floor, as a crumpled up thing in her chest?

Forgive me—I mean to say, you have left your mark on me.

But I already know, you have already made clear,

that I

am not

your world.

I Ask the Stars

Some nights I am surly with the stars, I ask,
are you even trying? Are you even looking?
Are you even listening? What are you doing
with all of my wishes if not granting them?
What are you doing with the power you've
been given? I need you, do you not want to be
needed? Do you not want to be loved? I have
jumped from need to love, I know, my fault,
the line between them is just so thin.

I ask, how can you hear me hope and plead
and beg and be so utterly umoved?

I ask the stars, I ask the stars.

(Only because I cannot ask you.)

It Doesn't

Missing you doesn't mean I forgive you
any more than
your silence means you're sorry.

Poetry

Hear me out—the years are short, but the days are long. No, listen—the days are short, but the nights are long. Wait, I've got this— life is short, but the days and nights are long.

This isn't poetry, this isn't poetry, this isn't poetry.

The love was short, but the heartbreak is long.

There we go.

Out of Stock

He comes here looking for a heart and I say I'm sorry sir, I'm sorry sir, I had one but it's out of stock. Tell you what, maybe the person who got it will return it. He didn't seem sold on it, so you never know, maybe he'll return it, but then maybe not, it's such a hassle to return things, especially when you won't get anything in exchange for it. Especially when he probably thinks I'll give him a hard time about bringing it back, when really I just want it to go to a good home. I can't stand the thought of it lying crumpled on his closet floor or in the cracks between his sofa cushions, I can't stand it.

I'm sorry sir, what I mean to say is—

if it comes back in, it's yours.

Burn This One

This was sweet once. Me, writing my silly stories. You, fighting your silly wars. Tying our weights to all the wrong things, like words could save us, like bullets could. Like there was something here worth saving. What were we that we are not now. I still clutch my pen, you still clutch your gun. We just fight for things that are not each other.

When I said I loved you, I meant I wanted to. When I say I wanted to, I mean despite it all, I chose to.

Burn this one, go ahead and burn it.

I already did.

A Hope of Poets

The first one most people think of is a murder of
crows, I think because it's sinister. A *murder* of
crows, a murder. An unkindness of ravens, that's
another favorite, though of all the unkindnesses
I have been shown, none have yet come from a
raven. A flight of sparrows, how fanciful. A
parliament of owls, how regal. What about
something that isn't a bird—perhaps a shrewdness
of apes. Have you ever heard of a huddle of
walruses, a rhumba of rattlesnakes? A glaring of
cats, how fitting.

What do you think they call a group of poets?

A heartbreak of poets, a loss of poets? A reach
of poets, a wanting of poets?

A hopelessness of poets, no—wait—a hope of poets.

Perhaps a hope of poets.

Dead Things

I buried our love in the dirt out back.

In the middle of the night, it calls to me.

Maybe dead things
don't know
they're dead.

Trapped

Love like a Chinese finger trap.

We can't come apart without
coming together first.

You are a thousand miles
away, and we

will never be free.

Something Someone Might Love

Lately I am a battle cry the world has muted. Every challenge I try to meet has already been met by someone else, and they're in *love*, ugh, they're in *love*. Who am I to stand in the way of love. Who am I, who am I, who the hell am I. I am a chaser of runners, a runner from chasers; a dreamer, a dream, *my* dream, someone's. I am a goddamn delight, I thought (he didn't.)

I practice smiling in my bedroom mirror, looking for some combination of teeth and curved lips that looks like something someone might love.

A friend texts me a joke, and when I look back up in the mirror I catch myself laughing.

I think I am already
something someone might love.

Careful

Are you careful with hearts since me?

I am careful with hearts since you.

With my own, I mean.

With my own.

My Bluff

I used to laugh and play and
howl at the moon like nothing
could hurt me, like no one
could hurt me, and you would
laugh and play and howl
alongside me, beside me,
colliding, joyriding, confiding
in me until the day

you called

my bluff.

The Bottom Line

I deserve better.

That's the bottom line, the very bottom line, the one I don't always read all the way down to. I get stuck at earlier lines, lines like "he cares about me" and lines like "he doesn't mean to hurt me."

But I've got the time now, your absence has given me the time now, to read all the way to the bottom, and

the bottom line is—

I did not deserve this.

Worth Something

Your words wrote checks
your actions couldn't cash.

What I mean to say is,
I'm still waiting for your promises
to be worth something.

So Many Reasons

You could've let me down gently but instead you dropped me, and—there aren't many reasons to lift something up high and then let it go, no, I can't think of many reasons except that maybe you forgot, yes, maybe you forgot to hold on, yes, or maybe it was me, maybe I slipped, maybe I slipped right through your fingers, yes, there could be so many reasons.

There could be so many reasons.

Like maybe you just like

to watch

things break.

The Far Away

I was mistaken in thinking
you couldn't hurt me from far away.

It turns out the far away
is what hurts me
most.

A Secret

Love is a secret the stars whispered
in our ears each night.

And I kept it.

I kept it even if
you didn't.

I Think You Know

My wanting you is tired. It curls up
inside of me, and oh, it is small, oh,
it did not used to be this small. I feel
the waning weight of it and think,
*I have wrestled yesterdays bigger
than this.* And I have—I live in
their shadow. (I did not win.)

If words alone could have saved us—

I think you know.

I think you know.

Free Trial

I got a free trial of love, but
I didn't cancel it in time.

And oh, I can't even tell you

how much

it cost me.

Borrowed Time

When I say that you and I
are on borrowed time, I mean
I have borrowed this time
from my own life, and it
cannot be returned.

And still I do not regret it.

An Hour Every Sunday

I let you have an hour every Sunday. It used to be all day, and before that, it used to be every day, but now I let you have any hour every Sunday. I think of your laugh and I do not fight it. I think of the weight of your chin on my head and I do not fight it. I think of you loving me and I do not fight it.

For an hour every Sunday.

Someday I will give you a minute, and

someday I won't give you anything.

But for now, I give you this.

By which I mean, for now—

I let myself have this.

Rib Cage Scaffolding

They say to open my heart, so I try a crowbar.
I try a lever, I try a screwdriver, I try a goddamn
sledgehammer. I would be proud of how
impenetrable I made it if it was something I'd
meant to do, but as it is, I did not intend to use
my rib cage as scaffolding for a fortress.

Someone suggests a key, but
I didn't build a door into these walls.

And even if I did, I know
some doors you think you have the keys to
still might never open.

Unfettered Hope

I have fed this body enough hurt. A steady diet of
he promised and *he wouldn't do this to me*. My heart's gone
heavy on unfettered hope, like a pig to slaughter, and
your silence makes a hell of an axe.

You know, loving you was a pit I had to
claw my way up out of.

It was something better once.

I swear, it was something better.

Sinking

I hoped your apology could save us,
but there were too many holes in it
for us to stay afloat.

In My Dream

In my dream you ask me if I'm
gone and I say *no, I'm right here,
you're the one who's gone.* You
laugh. You laugh and you say,
look at me. You laugh and you
say, *how can I be gone?*

And I echo it back, I echo it back.

I look at you and I say,

how can you be gone?

Joy

I have felt joy before, but I have never
known what to name it. How to hold it. Where
it goes when it goes, how to call it back, how to
keep it. I have called it by the names of men
who love me for a while, but when they go,
it goes; I think I'd do better naming it for me.

And yet! I whisper your name and here it is.

This is just to say—

I think you are very brave, and I would like

to love you.

I Keep Singing

I've watched enough medical shows to know that
sometimes you can't cut out the bad without
risking something good.

Sometimes they keep the patient awake on the table
during brain surgery and tell them to keep talking.

To keep singing.

I keep singing.

Just to make sure
that in losing you
I'm not also losing
me.

I Thought It Gave More

He said it takes too much to love me.

I guess I thought it gave

more.

The Trolley Problem

i stand still / i don't take a step / not a single
step / my feet are roots / my roots go miles /
miles deep / made of metal / made of steel / made
of wants i've sharpened into stakes / i don't pull
the lever / five people die instead of one / my
hands are clean / but dirty / clean / but dirty / i
stand still / i don't take a step / not a single step /

and it's the hardest thing

i've ever done.

Harbinger of Heartbreak

You are a harbinger of heartbreak. I know this
about you. I know you touch what you can't hold.
I know that—that? I called that love? Those
clumsy hands, that wasted smile? I called that
love? I know I called that love, but I don't know
how or why or who (who taught me that was love.)
We are the prologue, not the story. A cautionary
tale, not a fairy tale. Blinded more than blinding,
found me wanting more than wanted.

I don't reach for you anymore.

I don't reach for you anymore.

I don't reach for you anymore, though
with your eyes closed, you wouldn't know
either way.

How Shall I Put This

How shall I put this? I book rooms for an
extended stay, you book them by the
hour. I live for yesterdays and tomorrows,
you look beyond nothing but today. You
touch, I hold. I love, you want. I want, you
leave. You leave, I stay.

I am a student of heartbreak, and you
are the finest teacher I've ever known.

Long Gone

I know you better now that you're
long gone.

And the more I know you,
the less
I want to.

I Am Leaving That Piece Here

He asks why I have my shoes on, but I don't know, I don't remember putting them on. Both of us notice the suitcase at the same time, the one my two hands, I suppose, have packed without my knowledge. I am wearing a raincoat and I see now storm clouds gather; the thing in me that wants to go must have checked the forecast. You touch my hand but have already forgotten how to hold it, or I have forgotten how to let you. You kiss me, an ordinary kiss, but I call it a goodbye kiss in my head. Do you know I call it that. Do you know it *is* that. Do you know I don't want it to be. Do you know it is raining now. Do you know I am breaking now. Do you know when I woke this morning I watched you sleep for twenty minutes and imagined loving you for twenty years.

It isn't enough, though. Twenty minutes, twenty years. It isn't enough and it is raining now.

My hand is on the door. My foot is on the threshold. My eyes are on the sky. I love you. I love you.

I am leaving that piece here.

Fire Hazard

Loving you takes up too much space. Do you hear that? Do you hear me? Loving you is all of the boxes in my parents' basement they want me to go through because they're downsizing, except the basement is my heart and it's not getting any smaller.

Loving you has gotten dusty. (I mean foolish.) Mice have chewed the corners of loving you. (I mean hurt has.) I should rent a dumpster for all of this loving you. (I mean—no, I mean that.)

Do you hear that? Do you hear me?

I wasn't a risk until you made me one.

And now I'm a goddamn fire hazard.

They Were Wrong

They all told me you would call, but they were wrong. (They don't know you like I do.) They think you run on logic, not fear. They think you show you care by staying, not going. They think you mean the things you say when you say them, that you wouldn't say them otherwise. I hate to break it to them, one by one when they ask me about you. I hate to break it to them that you never called, you never called.

I hate to tell them they were wrong.

But mostly I hate that they were wrong.

It Was a Love Story

You left, and now no one calls it a love story
anymore. They call it a good faith effort, a
lesson learned. Sometimes, when they think
I cannot hear them, a mistake. What it was
has changed—the very bones of it, the sinews,
the filaments, the fibers, what your hand meant
on my hip, what mine meant on your cheek—
because of what it is—this. this. oh god this.

I suppose now that I am a woman, I was never
a child. Now that the sun has set, it was never
day. Now that the snow has melted, it was never
winter. Now that my heart is broken, it was never
whole.

It was a love story, it was a love story.

(Goddamnit, god*damn*it.)

Shipwreck

No one tells the shipwreck survivors they're clinging to the wreckage too tightly. When they finally make it to shore, no one tells them they survived all wrong. No one tells them they took too long getting there. No one tells them they were wrong to ever get on that ship. No one tells them to get right on the next ship.

When they ask me about you, I will say that I loved you too much.

But I will also say

that you never loved me

enough.

Trellis

Look, we just ran out of trellis.

A rose can only grow as high
as there's a structure to
support it.

We just ran out of trellis.

That doesn't mean we weren't beautiful.

Me and My Broken Heart

I am writing a buddy comedy called *Me
and My Broken Heart*, and in it, we get
in the car and go. My broken heart picks
the music. the destination. the color of
the sky. I pick the ways it breaks. It pushes
my foot down on the pedal and I say, *that's
dangerous, that's dangerous.* It doesn't care,
it's reckless, it's wrecked for less. For far
less. For nothing, for nothing at all.

We are Thelma and Louise, we
are Bonnie and Clyde, me and
my broken heart.

It breaks me but
I broke
it first.

Ashes

Everywhere else, I move on.

But here, between the four walls of
this page—

I clutch ashes.

I clutch ashes and I tell

the world of

the fire.

Unmade

What am I made of, I am made of the night
we met. Ships and starlight and sorrys, so
sorrys. I am made of a lost that comes after
found instead of the other way around. Firsts
and fingerprints and forgetting, I mean,
forgotten. (And fear.) (And fear.) I am made of
something someone wanted, or I was, once.
Thorns and teardrops and timing—the wrong
kind, did you know there was a wrong kind.

I am made of the night you left.

By which I mean I am

unmade by it.

I Blame You

You bandage my wounds and we
don't talk about how I got them.

There's a howl in my chest in the shape of your name.

Three years from now you leave me and
everyone sees it coming except me.

You blame my heart
for being made of glass.

I blame you
for dropping it.

About Hearts

I don't believe that how you treated
my heart says as much about how
you feel about me as it does
how you feel about hearts.

About hearts, about hearts, about your own heart.

It is worth more than you think.

And so was mine.

Tell Me

Tell me about a time you loved someone. Tell me about a night you didn't sleep, and why, and all the reasons you never regretted it. Tell me about a dream you didn't want to wake from, and why it was hard to leave it, and how your heart was broken, I'm sorry, I'm just assuming your heart was broken. Tell me about a dandelion wish that turned into a fallen star wish that turned into a birthday candle wish, which is to say a wish you didn't know how to stop wishing. Tell me about a morning you woke up and didn't want to be somewhere else. anywhere else. anyone else. Tell me about a joy you held and how carefully you held it. Tell me if it mattered. I need to know if it mattered. Tell me please tell me it mattered.

Tell me about a time you loved someone.

Tell me please tell me it mattered.

Runner

Somebody complimented my running time and
asked if I ran in college, and I said no, and I said
no, I did not run in college.

But I have run from all the boys
who ever tried to love me.

And I have run after

the one

who didn't.

Island

The summer I loved you, the river couldn't hold all the rain. Do you remember the way the street flooded. Do you remember smiling down at me and saying that the sky had gifted us an island. We made plans, half-joking, to use sticks to spell *don't save us* outside in the backyard. We made plans, half-serious, to toss our phones into the rising water so nothing could make us less of an island. We dragged the comforter downstairs and made a fort beneath the couch cushions, and you loved me, and I loved you.

Do you remember, do you remember.

You loved me, and

I loved you, and

nobody

could save us.

When It Tells Me

If a tree falls in the forest, and
nobody is there to hear it, I will
still always believe it.

When it tells me that it fell,

and when

it tells me that

it hurt.

Shallow Grave

I dug us too shallow a grave, and things
keep digging us up.

Things like your smile.

Things like my heart.

Things like memories—memories like a spade, like
a shovel, like two desperate cupped hands.

Truth be told, I don't know how to bury us

any more than you

knew how not to.

In Any Version

I have tried to write our story from
a hundred different angles, but no
matter how I approach it, I write us
into a corner.

Because I always want it to end happily.

But I can't find anything happy
in any version
where you and I end.

I Wish

I wish I could say
it got easier, but
no, I've just learned
to live with
how hard it is.

No Self-Preservation

I still love you sometimes, but like I still love candy after getting a cavity filled or like I still love tequila after waking up the next morning with no memory of the night before.

Like I have no self-preservation, like I get off on the pain.

Like I can't help it.

I mean, like I can but like I

don't want to.

Slow Burn

I don't do slow burn, nothing in me burns slowly. I catch a spark like nobody's business, like nobody's goddamn business, don't look at me, *don't look at me*. I reach with both hands to catch the sparks not meant for me and I go up like kindling, like tinder and twigs, all foolish flames and brazen blaze and snapping and crackling and *breaking* and *breaking*.

I burn for you, you know. you know. you know.

(Like nobody's goddamn business.)

Rebuilt

A wrecking ball has never rebuilt
a house that it destroyed.

Scissors have never glued pages
back inside a book.

An axe has never planted
a giant redwood tree.

I have stopped believing that
the hands that broke me
will put me back together.

The Sword in the Stone

These days, my heart is the
sword, my rib cage is the stone.

Now if you want it, you're
going to have to work for it.

Now if you want it, you're
going to have to be
worthy of it.

Right / Wrong

There is a wrong way to love
someone, and there is a wrong
way to leave them.

And if you get one wrong, I'm not
sure you ever stand a chance
of getting the other right.

Look At Me

Everything inside of me is busy keeping my heart from knowing that you're gone. My lungs keep inhaling, keep exhaling, thumbs up like *nothing to see over here*. Like *not drowning, no, most certainly not drowning*. My tear ducts stay dry, and something inside of me is still actively producing laughter. It even sounds real, so I'm proud of whatever it is, whatever is pulling this off. It's a stage production with next to no budget, but look at it go, look at me smile, look at me walking around, look at me, look at me, oh god why won't you

look at me.

My brain is like a parent trying to ease their child into knowing their goldfish is dead.

He's just sleeping honey, they say first.

He'll change his mind, my brain says first.

He's gone to swim in the ocean, they say next.

He needs some time, my brain says next.

Usually it's much later when the child realizes.

And it's even later when the heart does.

Do Me a Favor

I cannot forgive you,
so do me a favor
and at least let me
forget you.

I Just Want

How do I write poetry?

I wish I could say
something profound but
I just want.

I just want.

I just want
something badly enough
to stop everything and try
to write the words in which
I'll find it.

Empty All Along

You hand me nice words. Polished, shined, beautiful
words I turn over and over every night before falling
asleep. Treasured words I don't show anyone else
because I'm worried they'll lose their value if I see
them through someone else's eyes. Because I'm
worried they'll hold them up to the light and find
some flaw in them. (I don't want to find
a flaw in them.)

But eventually out of curiosity (another word
for desperation) I shake them
to see what lies
inside them.

And I find out
they've been empty
all along.

Anymore

The only thing more sad
than someone who doesn't dream

is someone who doesn't dream
anymore.

Some Wounds

At night I hold a shadow and call it by
your name. (No one else calls this
love.) Tree branches tap at my window,
and I pretend I'm very busy. *"Not now,
sweetheart, not now."* I pretend. I
pretend. I silence my phone and you
call every second I don't look at it.
(The longer I don't look at it, the more
true this might be.) I know you not
looking me in the eye has more to do
with you than it does with me, but it
hurts all the same and—

some wounds time can't heal.

I wish I didn't know that.

My Poem

This is my poem, and in it, no one dies young. Cars swerve at the last second. Bullets fall to the ground, impotent, the second they leave the barrel. Knives are all rubber. Angry words die in throats, decompose, regrow as sweet ones. There's no such thing as an endangered animal—they all live happy, they all live free, they all live. Everyone has enough. Enough what? Enough. Everyone falls in love, and no one falls back out of it.

Women walk home at night without their keys tucked between their fingers, and we stopped global warming in time—we cared enough.

Maybe that's all this world is, here in my poem—

we care enough.

Stacking Boxes

I have been stacking boxes
of sadness up against the walls
of my heart. I will go through
them later, I promise I will go
through them later.

But for now, I'd like
to make some room
for hope.

New Suitcase

I got a new suitcase.

Your hands have never touched this one, never lifted it into the back of your truck, you've never watched me sit on the floor of your bedroom and pack this one while you searched for something to say.

I've never stuffed this one with regrets and shoved it under my bed where I couldn't hear them scream.

I got a new suitcase, but that doesn't mean
I didn't keep the old one.

I let it scream.

(I let it remind me you once loved me.)

I Hold Nothing

I say you have a hold on me, but you don't,
you let go, no part of you holds me. Nor do
I have a hold on you, I have no hold, my hands
are empty, I have no you.

We had a hold on each other and now
I hold nothing and you hold nothing

but the power to

keep breaking me.

Status Update
(after Rebecca Lindenberg)

Kristina Mahr is here again. Is here still. Is absolutely aware she has not moved. Has grown roots, possibly, but is hoping nobody's noticed. Is lying. Is hoping *he's* noticed. Is hoping he's noticed she's still here. Is hoping he doesn't think she's just waiting around for him, but is hoping he's looked over his shoulder and realized she is still close enough to touch. Loves him, the fool. Hasn't drawn a breath since the day she met him without loving him, the fool. Kristina Mahr is wishing again. Is wishing the same wishes again. Is tired. Is tired of wishing the same wishes again. Kristina Mahr is wearing that black dress and downing a bottle of Miller Lite and laughing and laughing and standing in an alley and telling him not to kiss her again. Kristina Mahr is dreaming again, I mean. Is here again. Is here still.

Goldmine

I put on my helmet, I pick up my pickaxe. (By which I mean I remind myself it's better this way and pick up my pen.) I go into this wound like it's a mine and I'm searching for gold, but I'm just looking for poetry. Chiseling it from the walls of hurt. Collecting it in buckets like it was ever meant to see the light.

My heart is the canary.

It tells me when it's time to go.

It says this place

will kill me.

Wound / Wound

In the poem this isn't, your fingers are *wound* in my hair. My cheeks *match* the red of your shirt as I *lie* down beside you. Love is a roll of the *die*, and we won it. I need you like a *desert* needs rain. Everyone else comes *second* to you. There should be a *fine* for being this happy.

In the poem this is, you made a *wound* in my heart. You lit a *match* that burned everything we were to the ground, and you *lie*. you *lie*. you *lie*. You chose to *desert* us at the first opportunity, and you were gone in a *second*, the blink of an eye.

And I pretend that I am *fine*.

Over Me

I have not stopped
choosing you,

but I have stopped
choosing you
over me.

Fire
(A Nonet)

Is fire one syllable or two?
See, there I chose to make it two.
Later, though, when they ask me
how it felt to lose you,
I will have to make
it one: it felt
like my heart
was on
fire.

The Light

I want to be your way, the way you go, privy to the
way you are. I want to listen to all my friends
complain about their significant others and not
have a goddamn thing to contribute, but I won't be
smug about it, I swear I won't be smug about it, you
know you aren't any more perfect than I am. Yes you
leave your dishes in the sink for days and yes you use
up all the hot water and yes you have the worst taste
in sweaters—but nothing in me hurts from loving
you. The dishes in the sink aren't broken. You write *I
love you* on the mirror in the shower steam, and you
give me your hideous sweaters to wear when I'm cold.
Without hesitation, without thought.

When I say I love you, I mean
the sky is no longer the color
I thought it was.

I mean I thought the stars
were puncture holes.

I mean I can finally hold
the light.

Someone New to Blame

If this is all a simulation, I humbly request a
rewind. Humbly, so humbly, I beg on my knees
to go back. I will not get on that plane, why did
I get on that plane, I humbly ask if I can blame you
for me getting on that plane. I've been looking
for someone new to blame. Someone pressed
the wrong button. Someone fell asleep at the
controls. I fell in love and he left. I fell in love
and he left. I fell in love and he left. Do you
not see. Are you not watching the thing you
built. I've been screaming at the stars but I
could be screaming at you.

I fell in love and he left.

I will only ever scream at you
for one of those.

You Didn't Mind

When something falls / I try to catch it / I don't want it to break / I don't want to break it / when I fell / you didn't try to catch me / you didn't mind me breaking / you didn't mind breaking me.

I won't chase after
the things / that don't want me
anymore.

Nor will I chase after
the things / that want me but
are cowards.

Shadow Boy

In my memories you are not real. Shadow boy.
Blurred boy. Ghost boy. Sometimes you have eyes,
sometimes you have lips, depending on the memory.
You always have a laugh, somehow you always have
a laugh. In one you have one hand. In one you
have both. In one you have nothing but
a heartbeat. a heartbeat. a heartbeat.

In one you have kindness.

In one you have cruelty.

In one you forget
to ever come back.

Special Problems in Vocabulary
(after Tony Hoagland)

There is no word for what love becomes when it dies. When a person dies, their soul leaves their body, but when love dies, what leaves what. (What leaves who.) (Who leaves who.) There is no word for where love goes when it's gone. Nobody says it's in a better place. Nobody can tell you where it went. It just goes, it's just gone. You can ask, you can beg, but it just left, just move on.

There is no word for what a rose becomes when it dies, when it becomes all thorns, no petals.

But I know it's not a rose anymore.

I know I can't call it a rose anymore.

A Soft Spot

Scar tissue has about
eighty percent of the strength
of normal tissue.

What I'm saying is, I have a soft spot for you still.

It was love and then

an open wound and now

a scar.

To Live One

I have lived whole lives
in your absence,
but I would give them all back
to live one
in your presence.

Among the Clouds

When I run, it is for the hills. I am unstoppable when I run, once I start running.

It takes me a long time to get going.

I need a push.

A push.

Usually my feet drag the first couple steps, but

if you keep pushing,

I will run.

I will run so far you will never find me.

I will build a life in these hills.

I will live among
the clouds.

Heart, Broken

I am not heartbroken.

I am not a heart, broken.

I have a heart, broken.

But I am not this brokenness.

I am what
           will heal it.

Forget-Me-Nots

Hurt is a trench I duck down into. They tell me
to use it, but then they don't like how I use it. I
know what they wanted, look, I know what they
wanted. They wanted me to toss seeds down
into it, they wanted me to water them, they
wanted something to grow. Something beautiful
like roses, like forget-me-nots, like I need any
goddamn thing to help me forget you not.
But I'm no fool, in this I'm no fool. There's such
a thing as holes too deep. Nothing I plant in
these holes would ever reach the sun. Nothing
that goes in them is ever coming back out as
something beautiful.

So I put fence posts in them. I use them, these
holes like trenches, so deep they can hold
a post ten miles high.

I build walls from hurt and dream of
all the ways they might
have saved me.

We Blame the Stars

We do not break when dawn does. We fall from grace and for each other's hands and lips and eyes, walking the fine and finer line between a promise and a lie. We swore we wouldn't be this but we are this, we become this—looking for and past and through each other, grown numb to this, we succumb to this. We squeeze words free from between clenched teeth, and only small ones make it through. We swallow down the bigger ones, the sweet ones, the *I love you*s.

We fight, this time against instead of for— and when it ends, we blame the stars.

We blame
the goddamn
stars.

i do not carry your heart with me
(after e.e. cummings)

i do not carry your heart with me (i thought i carried your heart with me) i am always without it (where did i lose it, how did i lose it) and whatever i do in this life is because you left me (the broken things, the brilliant things)

i do not fear my fate (for i no longer believe in fate) and every world in which i walk is one without you in it (i was wrong to think the world was you and you, the world) and the moon says i was mistaken in thinking it meant you and the sun says i misheard your name within the song it tried to sing

here is the deepest secret everyone knows but me (here is the tangled root of a felled tree in a dying forest beneath a cursed sky in this life we thought we'd build together;which does not grow, will never again grow) and this is the wonder that's keeping the stars from shining

i do not carry your heart with me (i thought i carried your heart with me)

At a Price

In a world where words cost money, I catch
him counting out his change before he tells
me I look beautiful. Three weeks pass before
he saves up enough to tell me that he
misses me when I'm gone, and three more
pass before he tells me he is falling for me.

When he tells me that he loves me, I hug the
words close to my chest. I feel their weight, I
see their shine, no cheap knockoffs here. (Not
like I've been handed in the past.)

In a world where words cost money, each
word comes at a price, and so
each word comes with care.

(In this world, only one of those is true.)

A Thing You Hold

"—perchance to dream." To dream. To dream. To come out the other side of darkness. To remember—for next time—that it has an other side. To keep walking toward the things you cannot see. To call the sunrise by its name—a miracle. To let it wake you. To let it keep waking you. To look at your own hands. No—to see them. To see what they can hold instead of only what they have held. To stand beneath the night and let it be a thing you hold.

To be missed by those you miss. No—to know it.

To be missed by those you miss and to be loved by those you love and yes—

to know it.

Perchance to dream. Perchance to let it be

a thing you hold.

The Ways We Fall

Do you know what falling feels like?

First you fall for (each other.) You fall head
over heels, you fall deep. You fall

in love.

Then you fall away (from each other.) You fall
silent, you fall apart. You fall

out of love.

Did you know that falling can feel like flying?

Did you know
that falling can feel like
        dying.

Petals

A thing I thought
was dead is growing
petals.

I watched it die, I watched
it die.

I see now I should have
burned it to
the ground.

Then I Defy You, Stars

You don't need me and I don't
need you, but we want each
other terribly. Terribly, terribly
well, terribly beautifully. When
you say my name, you push
its eight letters together so
hard that it ignites. I have never
before caught sparks on
someone's tongue. I have never
before been shown the heat of
my own fire. Nobody before has
ever held me like remembrance,
like the abolition of forgetting.

I defy the space between us like
Romeo defied the stars.

Like I have fallen to my knees before it.

Like I will not let it break us.

Like it might break us all the same.

CONTENTS

A Blessing	131
A Buffer, A Barrier	62
A Delicate Thing	29
A Hope of Poets	144
A Lake Somewhere	78
A Mess	11
A Pocket of Air	67
A Race	99
A Secret	154
A Soft Spot	213
A Thing You Hold	221
A Waiting	71
About Hearts	180
All for You	40
All New Songs	2
All or None	7
Always Always	18
Always Going, Always Gone	137
Among the Clouds	215
An Hour Every Sunday	158
And to Think	21
Any Greater	82
Anymore	197
Anywhere, Anything, Anyone	56
Are You Coming Back	47
Ashes	177
At a Price	220
Be Kind	42
Because It's Sad	91
Borrowed Time	157
Both You and Peace	92
Burn This One	143
Can You Believe It	125
Careful	148
Champagne Promises	55

Crushed	20
Darkness	90
Dead Things	145
Deep Down	6
Do Me a Favor	194
Dormant	37
Empty All Along	196
Even the Bad Ones	101
Every Day	100
Everything Everything	115
Fire	207
Fire Hazard	171
For as Long as I Can	94
Forbid Me	133
Forget-Me-Nots	217
Forgive Me	60
Formative Memory	126
Free Trial	156
From the Jaws of Catastrophe	135
Go Ahead and Ask Me	28
Goldilocks	53
Goldmine	204
Gone With the Wind	121
Guarantees	98
Guessing	107
Harbinger of Heartbreak	167
Hard to Get	124
Heart, Broken	216
How Long	14
How Shall I Put This	168
How Was I Supposed to Know	93
I Am Leaving That Piece Here	170
I Am Not Wrong About This	19
I Ask the Stars	139
I Blame You	179
I Can't Escape You	68
I Did Not Know	136

i do not carry your heart with me	219
I Hold Nothing	202
I Just Want	195
I Keep Singing	164
I Think You Know	155
I Thought It Gave More	165
I Will Not	35
I Wish	187
I Wish You Really Had It	108
I'll Run Again	39
If Given the Chance	86
If You Wonder Why	17
If You're Looking	132
Imagine If	102
In a Crowd	85
In Any Version	186
In My Dream	162
Instead I Know	106
Instead of Peace	49
Irreparable	26
Is It?	48
Island	183
It Doesn't	140
It Is	128
It Was a Love Story	173
Joy	163
Just Another Thing	24
Just Fine	88
Just Like That	130
Just Words	10
Least Of All Me	104
Like an Anvil	80
Long Gone	169
Look At Me	193
Love Wins	105
Maybe I Was Right	70
Me and My Broken Heart	176

Meant to Be	114
Memories Included	129
Mime on a City Street Corner	76
More With You	30
My Bluff	149
My Love Language Must Be	22
My Own	116
My Poem	199
My To-Do List	54
My Tricky Love	119
Needle & Thread	134
New Suitcase	201
Next	75
No Blood	127
No Self-Preservation	188
Not Even	117
Not Here	34
Not One	112
On My Wall	96
On the Roadside	12
Our Story	64
Out of Stock	142
Outlier	113
Over Me	206
Over This	111
Petals	223
Planted Dreams	69
Plenty of Fish	84
Poem Fodder	4
Poetry	141
Poetry Doesn't Care	73
Reappraised	97
Rebuilt	190
Repeat the Sounding Joy	63
Rib Cage Scaffolding	159
Right / Wrong	192
Runner	182

Shadow Boy	211
Shallow Grave	185
Shipwreck	174
Sinking	161
Sisyphus	87
Slow Burn	189
Small	110
So I Walk	51
So Incomplete	123
So Long	79
So Many Reasons	152
So Much More	45
So Much Space	58
Solar Flare	25
Some Wounds	198
Someone New to Blame	209
Something Someone Might Love	147
Something That Can Leave You	27
Something to Be Remembered	95
Special Problems in Vocabulary	212
Stacking Boxes	200
Status Update	203
Sticks and Stones	122
Still	120
Still Waiting	103
Swept Up	59
Tell Me	181
Ten Thousand Piece Puzzle	89
The Audacity of Heartbreak	83
The Big Bang	118
The Bottom Line	150
The Far Away	153
The Light	208
The Only Place	9
The Past	33
The Poor Souls	46
The Second	31

The Sword in the Stone	191
The Trolley Problem	166
The Ways We Fall	222
The Why	5
The World is Ending	36
Then I Defy You, Stars	224
There Was a Time	57
They Were Wrong	172
Things That Used to Be Walls	65
This Knowing	32
Threadbare	74
Three for Three	109
Threw Out	81
To Live One	214
Tomorrow	50
Trapped	146
Trellis	175
Try As I Might	61
Unfettered Hope	160
Unfinished Business	15
Unmade	178
Untouched Snow	77
Waiting	8
We Blame the Stars	218
What I Mean	52
What It's Supposed To	72
What Would You Do	44
When It Tells Me	184
When Something Hurts	41
When They Ask Me	16
Who Will	43
Without a Scratch	1
Worth	3
Worth Something	151
Wouldn't You Know	66
Wound / Wound	205
Yarn	13

You Didn't Mind	210
You Would	38
Your Own Ringtone	23
Your World	138

ACKNOWLEDGMENTS

This collection is for all of the usual suspects—my family, my friends, my wonderful readers, etc—and then it is also, most especially, for my fellow writers.

You are doing a brave thing every time you put words on a blank page. It might not feel like it at the time. It might feel scary, it might feel pointless, it might feel like a waste of time. It isn't. It won't be.

I am still convinced that words will save us.

We just have to let them.

ABOUT THE AUTHOR

Kristina Mahr devotes her days to numbers and her nights to words. She works full-time as an accountant in the suburbs of Chicago, but her true passion is writing. In her spare time, she enjoys spending time with her family, friends, and small herd of rescue animals, as well as waking up at the crack of dawn every weekend to watch the Premier League.

You can find more information about her other poetry collections, as well as her fiction novels on her website at:

www.kristinamahr.com

Printed in Great Britain
by Amazon